32d Congress, 1st Session. | [H. OF REPS.] | Ex. Doc. No. 25.

UTAH.

MESSAGE

FROM THE

PRESIDENT OF THE UNITED STATES,

TRANSMITTING

Information in reference to the condition of affairs in the Territory of Utah.

January 9, 1852.

Referred to the Committee on Territories, and ordered to be printed.

To the House of Representatives:

In answer to the resolution of the House of Representatives of the 15th ultimo, requesting information in regard to the Territory of Utah, I transmit a report from the Secretary of State, to whom the resolution was referred.

MILLARD FILLMORE.

Washington, *January* 9, 1851.

Department of State,
Washington, January 8, 1852.

The Secretary of State, to whom has been referred the resolution of the House of Representatives of the 15th ultimo, requesting the President to communicate to that House all such information as "may be in his possession, calculated to show the actual condition of things in the Territory of Utah, and especially to enable the House to ascertain whether the due execution of the laws of the United States has been resisted or obstructed; whether there has been any misapplication of the public funds; and whether the personal rights of our citizens have been interfered with in any manner,"—has the honor to lay before the President the papers mentioned in the subjoined list, which contain all the information in this department called for by the resolution.

Respectfully submitted:

DAN. WEBSTER.

To the President of the United States.

LIST OF PAPERS

Accompanying the report of the Secretary of State to the President, of the 8th of January, 1852.

Mr. Bernhisel to the President of the United States, with enclosures, December 1, 1851.

Mr. Snow to the President of the United States, September 22, 1851.

Governor Young to the President of the United States, October 20, 1851.

Report of Messrs. Brandebury, Brocchus, and Harris, to the President of the United States, December 19, 1851.

Mr. Harris to Mr. Webster, January 2, 1852.

Mr. Harris to the President, with enclosures, January 2, 1852.

Mr. Bernhisel to the President of the United States, December 30, 1851.

Governor Young to the President of the United States, September 29, 1851.

Memorial signed by members of the Legislative Assembly of Utah to the President of the United States, September 29, 1851.

From John M. Bernhisel, esq., Delegate from Utah Territory, to the President.

United States Hotel,
December 1, 1851.

Sir: Agreeably to your request, I have the honor to inform you that the news of the organization of the Territory of Utah was most gratefully received by its inhabitants. The news of the passage of the bill establishing the government, and the appointment under it of officers, executive and judicial, reached Great Salt Lake City about Christmas or New Year last, and was greeted by the firing of cannon and every other demonstration of enthusiastic joy. The governor took the oath of office soon afterwards, but the Territory was not fully organized until the beginning of August. The 4th of July, the last glorious anniversary of our independence, was celebrated at Great Salt Lake City with considerable eclat. The officers not residents of the Territory reached the scene of their duties a fortnight after, on the 19th of July, with the exception of Judge Perry C. Brocchus.

The officers were all respectfully and hospitably received. They showed themselves pleased with the condition of the Salt Lake settlement, and the comforts which the industry of its inhabitants had gathered around them in their Alpine home; although they found the California prices which prevail there, and the expenses of living under them, incommensurate with the rate of salary granted them by the United States. At their request, therefore, I am the bearer of a petition, of which I enclose you a copy, praying Congress for an increased remuneration. And though as yet, owing to the pacific character of our people, no case is known to have occurred which may invoke the action of the court or its officers, this request will not, perhaps, be deemed unreasonable. I left Utah Territory upon the first of September last. Up to that date the harmony and peace prevailing between the different officers of the Government and the people continued undisturbed. The only statements that I have seen to the contrary appear to be based upon a letter enclosed, which has appeared in some of the public prints, purporting to have been written by a judicial officer of the Government, and dating from Salt Lake City, September 20, 1851. As I have as yet received no mail from the Territory, nor any information of any kind about its affairs since my departure, I am left to the letter alone for the evidence which it contains, and to this I beg to refer you with some attention. It declares that "not only were the officers sent here treated with coldness and disrespect, but that the Government of the United States, on all public occasions, whether festive or religious, was denounced in the most disrespectful terms, and often with invectives of great bitterness;" and proceeds to mention two instances to substantiate this statement.

At the occasion first named, the celebration of the 24th of July, the *putative* writer (If I may employ the expression) was not present. Judge Brocchus did not arrive in the Territory till the 17th of August. But I was present. I had the privilege of listening to Governor Young's remarks attentively, and therefore *know* that he made no reflections injurious to the public services or private character of the late lamented President Taylor, or in fact any allusions to him whatever, that I can remember. The writer's statement, therefore, is so far untrue.

The second "*instance*" also is open to correction. Its statement is, that the writer being commissioned by the Washington Monument Society to procure for them a block of marble, apprized Governor Young of the trust committed to his hands, and expressed a desire to address the people *on the subject*, when assembled in their greatest number; that the governor, in order to accede to his request, upon the Monday following, "*respectfully and honorably introduced*" him for the purpose to a meeting of at least three thousand people; that he spoke for two hours, during which he was favored with the unwavering attention of his audience; but that he then, by his own statement, "incidentally thereto (as the Mormons supposed") attacked the governor and people, and concluded by what they cannot but have taken as a most wanton insult, "that if they would not offer a block of marble in full fellowship with the people of the United States, as brethren and fellow-citizens, they had better not offer it all, but leave it unquarried in the bosom of its native mountain." I do not remark upon this strange mode of springing an insult upon a public meeting, after its patience had been tried by a *two hours'* oration; impolitic, one would think, in a judicial officer, desirous to keep the peace, or an agent of the Washington Monument Society, wishing to obtain a tribute to the memory of the Father of his Country, but merely ask you to observe that the public attack of the "judicial officer" upon the governor of the Territory, appears also to have been based upon Mr. Young's alleged expressions upon the memory of General Taylor, which certainly were not cast upon the occasion to which I have already adverted.

The letter-writer states, moreover, that at the celebration of the 24th of July, "the orator of the day spoke bitterly of the course of the United States towards the Church of Latter Day Saints, in taking a battalion of men from them for the war with Mexico, while on the banks of the Missouri river, in their flight from the mob at Nauvoo; that the government had devised the most wanton, cruel, and dastardly means for the accomplishment of their ruin, overthrow, and utter extermination; at which time also Governor Young denounced, in the most sacrilegious terms, President Taylor." I again repeat, the writer of the preceding extract was not present at the celebration to which he refers. There were some ten or twelve orators on that occasion, and the whole day was occupied by their speeches; but I heard no such language as I have quoted, nor any other which could be construed into the slightest disrespect towards the Government of the United States. All the officers of the government who were then in the Territory dined with the governor on that day. I am not aware that a single incident occurred to mar its gaiety and good fellowship.

The government *did not* TAKE from us a battalion of men, but one of its most gallant officers made a call for volunteers, and Mr. Young said in reply: "You shall have your battalion at once, if it has to be a class of our elders." More than five hundred able-bodied men promptly responded to the call, leaving their wives and children on the plains, and five hundred teams without drivers, and rendered efficient service in the war with the Mexican republic.

When I took my departure from Utah, the architect of the contemplated capitol was busily employed in preparing the plans and drawings for the building, and the governor was very desirous that they should be completed, and a daguerreotype of them taken to be exhibited by me to the President and members of Congress, in order that they might see what kind of building it was proposed to erect. But it was not designed to commence the erection of the building until the ensuing spring.

I have the honor to be, very respectfully and truly, your most obedient servant,

JOHN M. BERNHISEL,
Delegate from Utah.

To the PRESIDENT OF THE UNITED STATES.

[Printed slip enclosed with Mr. Bernhisel's communication to the President.]

Extract of a letter from a judicial officer of the government, at Great Salt Lake City, dated September 20, 1851.

I shall leave for the States on the 1st October; and most gladly will I go, for I am sick and tired of this place, of the fanaticism of the people, followed by their violence of feeling towards the "*gentiles*," as they style all persons not belonging to their church. I have had a feeling and personal proof of their fanatical intolerance within the last few days. I will give you a cursory view of the circumstances and the scene.

As soon after my arrival here as my illness would permit, I heard from Judge B. and Mr. Secretary H. accounts of the intolerant sentiments of the community towards government officers and the government itself, which filled me with surprise. I learned that not only were the officers sent here treated with coolness and disrespect, but that the Government of the United States, on all public occasions, whether festive or religious, was denounced in the most disrespectful terms, and often with invectives of great bitterness. I will mention a few instances. The 24th July is the anniversary of the arrival of the Mormons in this valley. It was on that day of this year that they assembled to commemorate that interesting event. The orator of the day, on that occasion, spoke bitterly of the course of the United States towards the church of "*Latter Day Saints*," in taking a battallion of their men from them for the war with Mexico, while on the banks of the Missouri river, in their flight from the mob at Nauvoo. He said the Government of the United States had devised the most wanton, cruel, and dastardly means for the accomplishment of their ruin, overthrow, and utter extermination.

His Excellency Governor Young, on the same occasion, denounced, in the most sacrilegious terms, the memory of the illustrious and lamented general and President of the United States, who has lately gone to the grave, and over whose tomb a nation's tears have scarcely ceased to flow. He exclaimed, "*Zachary Taylor is dead and gone to hell, and I am glad of it!*" and his sentiments were echoed by a loud amen from all parts of the assembly. Then, rising in the excess of his passion to his tiptoes, he vociferated, "*I prophesy, in the name of Jesus Christ, by the power of the priesthood that is upon me, that any other President of the United States, who shall lift his finger against this people, will die an untimely death and go to hell.*" This kind of feeling I found pervading the whole community, in some individuals more marked than in others.

You may remember that I was authorized by the managers of the Washington National Monument Society to say to the people of the Territory of Utah, that they would be pleased to receive from them a block of marble or other stone, to be deposited in the monument "*as an offering at the shrine of patriotism.*" I accordingly called on Governor Young, and apprized him of the trust committed to my hands, and expressed a desire to address the people upon the subject, when assembled in their greatest number. He replied that on the following Monday the very best opportunity would be presented. Monday came, and I found myself at their Bowery, in the midst of at least three thousand people. I was respectfully and honorably introduced by "*His Excellency*" to the vast assemblage. I made a speech, though so feeble that I could scarcely stand, and staggered in my debility several times on the platform.

I spoke for two hours, during which time I was favored with the unwavering attentions of my audience. Having made some remarks in reference to the judiciary, I presented the subject of the National Monument, and *incidently thereto* (as the Mormons supposed) I expressed my opinions in a full, free, unreserved, yet respectful and dignified manner, in regard to the defection of the people here from the Government of the United States. I endeavored to show the injustice of their feelings towards the Government, and alluded boldly and feelingly to the sacrilegious remarks of Governor Young towards the memory of the lamented Taylor. I defended, as well as my feeble powers would allow, the name and character of the departed hero, from the unjust aspersions cast upon them, and remarked that, in the latter part of the assailant's bitter exclamation that he "*was glad that Gen. Taylor was in hell,*" he did not exhibit a Christian spirit, and that if the author did not early repent of the cruel declaration, he *would perform that task with keen remorse upon his dying pillow.* I then alluded to my nativity; to my citizenship; to my love of country; to my duty to defend my country from unjust aspersions wherever I met them; and trusted that when I failed to defend her, my tongue, then employed in her advocacy and praise, might cling to the roof of my mouth, and that my arm, ever ready to be raised in her defence, might fall palsied at my side. I then told the audience if they could not offer a block of marble in a feeling of full fellowship with the people of the United States, as brethren and fellow-citizens, they had better not offer it at all, but leave it unquarried in the bosom of its native mountain. At the close of my speech the governor arose and denounced me and the Government in the most brutal and unmeasured terms.

The ferment created by his remarks was truly fearful. It seemed as if the people (I mean a large portion of them) were ready to spring upon me like hyenas and destroy me. The governor, while speaking, said that some persons might get their hair pulled or *their throats cut on that occasion.* His manner was boisterous, passionate, infuriated in the extreme; and if he had not been afraid of final vengeance, he would have pointed his finger at me, and I should *in an instant* have been a dead man. Ever since then the community has been in a state of intense excitement, and murmurs of personal violence and assassination towards me have been freely uttered by the lower order of the populace. How it will end I do not know. I have just learned that I have been denounced, together with the Government and officers, in the Bowery again to-day, by Governor Young. I hope I shall get off safely. God only knows. I am in the power of a desperate and murderous set. I however feel no great fear. So much for defending my country.

I expect all the officers of the Territory, at least Chief Justice B., Secretary Harris, and Captain Day, Indian agent, will return with me, *to return here no more.*

GREAT SALT LAKE CITY,
September 22, 1851.

SIR: For reasons satisfactory to themselves, Judges Brandebury and Brocchus, and Secretary Harris, leave this Territory for the States next week.

But I, for reasons satisfactory to myself, have thought best to write you a line, stating that after the causes which led to this unhappy event occurred, I used all my influence to bring about a reconciliation, but failed.

Did my sense of duty require me to return without consulting you, the duties I owe to my little family would forbid my undertaking the journey so late in the season. Should you, or Congress, on inquiry into the facts, be of the opinion that I also ought to return, that opinion can be made known to me, and it shall then be done according to your wishes.

I forbear to state the facts for the reason that Judges Branderbury and Brocchus, and Secretary Harris, will see you in person, and also Doctor Bernhisel, delegate from Utah, who will be able to inform you much better than I can by letter.

It is proper to state that Doctor Bernhisel left here before the main facts occurred which led to this event; he, therefore, will have to be informed of them by the people here.

I have the honor to subscribe myself your obedient servant,

Z. SNOW.

To his Excellency MILLARD FILLMORE,
President of the United States.

GREAT SALT LAKE CITY,
October 20, 1851.

SIR: Owing to the peculiar situation of our Territory in relation to public officers, I presume again to address you a few lines. You will please to recollect, that at the close of my last communication the Legislative Assembly was still in session. It so continued until the third instant, at which time they adjourned until the first Monday in January next, when they will resume their sitting.

Upon the departure of Mr. Secretary Harris, and the two judges, Messrs. Brandebury and Brocchus, the Legislative Assembly proceeded to re-district the Territory, and assigned the remaining judge, the honorable Zerubabel Snow, to perform the duty of holding all the district courts in the Territory until other judges shall be appointed and enter upon the discharge of their duties.

Being extremely inconvenienced for the want of a secretary, and apprehending some considerable delay might occur before another would appear, I took the liberty of appointing one, to act in that office pro tem., until the disability should cease to exist, or the vacancy be filled by the President. Dr. Willard Richards is the gentleman I have so appointed, who would be a good selection for that office, if the President and Senate should feel inclined to favor him. The proceedings of the legislature will be forwarded as soon as they can be arranged in proper form.

I also beg leave to add, that upon Indian affairs I have never received any instructions; the Indian agent, Mr. Holeman, came here, but immediately left to attend a treaty at Laramie, which he had pre-engaged to do. He has not returned to this place since. Mr. Day accompanied the officers, and it is presumed that upon meeting with Mr. Holeman they all returned to the States together; no report has been received from any of them as yet, except Mr. Rose, who is now in this city. I shall report to the proper department, to which I refer you for further particulars. My object in mentioning this subject in this letter, is to keep you authenticated, in order that the proper instructions may be had in this superintendency.

The Indians are generally peaceable, with the exception of those on Mary's river, where it has become very unsafe to travel. Those Indians have never been under the influence of the settlers of this Territory. It is proposed by some of the citizens to make a settlement, and establish a trading post in the vicinity. If the heretofore favorable influence of such a proceeding shall in like manner be successful and prevail in that region, the desired security will be obtained, and the traveller, with the usual and necessary caution, can go in safety.

With sentiments of high esteem, I remain, sir, most truly, your humble servant,

BRIGHAM YOUNG,
Governor of Utah Territory.

To his Excellency MILLARD FILLMORE,
President of the United States.

Report of Messrs. Brandebury, Brocchus, and Harris, to the President of the United States.

WASHINGTON, *December* 19, 1851.

SIR: It becomes our duty, as officers of the United States for the Territory of Utah, to inform the President that we have been compelled to withdraw from the Territory, and our official duties, in consequence of an extraordinary state of affairs existing there, which rendered the performance of those duties not only dangerous, but impracticable, and a longer residence in the Territory, in our judgment, incompatible with a proper sense of self-respect, and the high regard due to the United States. We have been driven to this course by the lawless acts and the hostile and seditious feelings and sentiments of Brigham Young, the Executive of the Territory, and the great body of the residents there, manifested towards the Government and officers of the United States in aspersions and denunciations so violent and offensive as to set at defiance, not only a just administration of the laws, but the rights and feelings of citizens and officers of the United States residing there.

To enable the Government to understand more fully the unfortunate position of affairs in that Territory, it will be necessary to explain the extraordinary religious organization existing there—its unlimited pretensions, influence, and power; and to enter into a disagreeable detail of facts, and the language and sentiments of the governor and others high in authority, towards the Government, people, and officers of the United States.

We found upon our arrival that almost the entire population consisted of a people called Mormons; and the Mormon church overshadowing and controlling the opinions, the actions, the property, and even the lives of its members; usurping and exercising the functions of legislation and the judicial business of the Territory; organizing and commanding the military; disposing of the public lands upon its own terms; coining money, stamped

"Holiness to the Lord," and forcing its circulation at a standard fifteen or twenty per centum above its real value; openly sanctioning and defending the practice of polygamy, or plurality of wives; exacting the tenth part of every thing from its members, under the name of tithing, and enormous taxes, from citizens, not members; penetrating and supervising the social and business circles; and inculcating, and requiring, as an article of religious faith, implicit obedience to the counsels of "the Church," as paramount to all the obligations of morality, society, allegiance, and of law.

At the head of this formidable organization, styled "The Church of Jesus Christ of Latter Day Saints," stood Brigham Young, the governor, claiming, and represented to be, the Prophet of God, and his sayings as direct revelations from Heaven, commanding thereby unlimited sway over the ignorant and credulous. *His* opinions and wishes were *their* opinions and wishes. He was consulted by them, upon almost every subject, as an oracle. No man pretended to embark in any kind of business without his permission, or conciliating him by a deferential consultation. In a word, he ruled as he pleased, without a rival or opposition, for no man dared question his authority.

Congress having established a territorial government for this people, and extended the constitution and laws of the United States over them, we were not only anxious for a cordial coöperation of all the officers and people in the organization of the Territory and a faithful administration of the laws, but equally anxious to avoid everything in the execution of our duties that would be likely to exhibit a conflict between the government and the church. Our main reliance was upon Brigham Young, the governor, for no man else could govern them against his influence, without a military force. As he had sought, and been honored with the office of Executive of the Territory, we presumed he was well disposed towards the government, and would wield his unbounded influence to secure respect and obedience to the government and the laws.

But in this we were disappointed. He made us feel, upon our arrival in the Territory, in a manner that could not be mistaken, that he was jealous of his power as head of the church, and hostile to the government of the United States and its officers, coming there to perform this duty, under the organic act.

One of the undersigned (Chief Justice Brandebury) arrived in the Territory on the 7th of June, a month and more before any of the other officers from the States. He availed himself of the earliest day after his arrival not only to pay his respects to Governor Young, as Executive of the Territory, but to inform him that he was there ready to enter upon his official duties, and for that purpose invited the United States attorney, Mr. Blair, (a Mormon,) to accompany and introduce him. Before the hour arrived, however, on the day appointed, Mr. Blair called to say that the governor's engagements would prevent an interview that day, and proposed another time to call upon his Excellency. At the appointed time, another effort was made, in company with Mr. Blair, who led the way to the office occupied by the governor. The chief justice was requested to tarry upon the stairway until Mr. Blair advanced to open the door and make inquiry if the governor could be seen. He was anticipated, however, by the governor's clerk (an Englishman) meeting him at the door, and after a few words between them in an undertone, returned with the information that the governor was not in, and with many regrets for this second failure. Satisfied that this was the result

of design on the part of the governor, no further effort was made to see him. This conduct of the governor was known in the community, and afforded much merriment to some of the Mormons. We were informed afterwards that Mr. Blair had made several private applications to the governor to know if he would allow an interview to the chief justice, but he refused, declaring that "he did not wish an introduction, for none but Mormons should have been appointed to the offices of the Territory, and none others but d—d rascals would have come among them." We refer to this incident now, only to show the feelings of the governor towards the government and officers at this early period.

On the 19th of July, another of the undersigned (Secretary Harris) arrived, in company with Judge Snow and Messrs. Babbit, Bernhisel, Day, and Rose, the two last-named being Indian sub-agents. A few days afterwards, the secretary was invited by the governor to be present at an interview between him and Mr. Babbit. This interview was made the occasion of a violent exhibition of his temper and abuse of Mr. Babbit, and of the government and officers, "intended for the secretary," as the governor afterwards declared, "to let him know what kind of people he had to deal with." These were but manifestations of that hostile feeling, the murmurs and mutterings of which were rife throughout the community, and intended that it should not escape our ears.

Upon the occasion of celebrating the anniversary of the arrival of the Mormon pioneers into the Valley, (the 24th July,) an immense concourse of their people were assembled from all parts of the Territory. Those of us then in the Territory were invited to be present and participate in the festivities of the occasion. We were seated upon the stand or platform, with a number of the leading men of the church, including the present delegate in Congress, (Hon. John M. Bernhisel.) The governor rose to address the audience, and a profound silence ensued, as is always the case when he rises to speak. After reflecting in terms of condemnation upon the alleged hostility of General Taylor to the Mormons, and to giving them a government, he exclaimed, in a loud and exulting tone, "But Zachary Taylor is dead, and in hell, and I am glad of it." Then drawing himself up to his utmost height, and stretching his hands towards heaven, he declared in a still more violent voice, "and I prophesy in the name of Jesus Christ, by the power of the Priesthood that's upon me, that any President of the United States who lifts his finger against this people shall die an untimely death, and go to hell." To this sentiment there came up from those seated around us, and from all parts of the house, loud and mingled responses of "Amen!" "Good!" "Hear!"

With the invitation to be present on this occasion, was an invitation to dine with the governor. Although we believed the occasion of our presence was seized upon by the governor to show us how brave and independent he could be in his declarations, and with what impunity our feelings could be outraged and insulted, we were forced, from an indisposition to produce a rupture and break off our official relations so soon after our arrival, to smother our indignation and mingle in the parade of a dinner.

Upon a subsequent occasion, (the 6th of September,) in reply to the remarks made by one of the undersigned (Associate Justice Brocchus) upon the subject, before a large audience, the governor reiterated and declared, "I did say that General Taylor was dead and in hell: *and I know it*" A man in the crowd, seemingly to give the governor an opportunity of

fixing its truth, spoke out and said, "How do you know it?" To which the governor promptly answered, "Because God told me so." An Elder, second only to the governor in the church, (Heber C. Kimball,) laying his hand on the shoulder of Judge Brocchus, added, "Yes, Judge, and you'll know it, too; for you'll see him when *you* get there."

Upon the occasion before referred to, (24th of July,) another speaker, (D. H. Wells,) late chief justice of the State of Deseret, declared, that "in the winter of 1838–'39 the church was expelled from the State of Missouri by a murderous mob, under the exterminating order of Governor Lilburn W. Boggs;" that "in the year 1844, on the 27th day of June, the mob of Illinois murdered in cold blood the Prophet Joseph, and Patriarch Hyram Smith, while confined in jail under the guarantee of safety, and pledge of the governor, Thomas Ford;" and that when they had left their homes in 1846, in the most inclement season, and were pursuing their toilsome march westward, "the government of the United States required a battalion of five hundred men to leave their families in this precarious situation, without money, provisions, or friends, other than the God whom they serve, to perform a campaign of over two thousand miles, on foot, across trackless deserts and burning plains, to fight the battles of their country; even that country which had afforded them no protection from the ruthless ruffians who had plundered them of their property, robbed them of their rights, waylaid them in their peaceful habitations, and murdered them while under the safeguards of their pledged faith. That country that could have the *barbarity*, under such peculiar circumstances, to make such a requirement, could have no other object in view than to finish, by extermination, the work which had so ruthlessly begun."

Upon the same occasion, another speaker (W. W. Phelps, one of the "Regents of the University of Deseret") declared, as a just cause of hostility, that "the Mormons were proscribed by the United States—he had two wives, others of his brethren had more, and brother Brigham Young had still more, and none of them dare return to the United States with their families; for their dirty, mean, little, contracted laws would imprison them for polygamy."

Upon the following Sunday, the mayor of the city, Jedediah M. Grant, in eulogizing the strength of the Mormons, exultingly declared from the pulpit, in presence of one of the undersigned, (Mr. Harris,) "that now the United States could not conquer them by arms."

Brigham Young, the governor, announced, with great vehemence, from the stand and to individuals, while the feelings of the people were thus excited by such sentiments, "that he had ruled that people for years, and could rule them again; that the United States judges might remain in the Territory and draw their salaries, but they should never try a cause if he could prevent it."

Another speaker, already referred to, standing second in the church, (Heber C. Kimball,) encouraged by the example set him by the governor, declared, in a speech at a public meeting, "that the United States officers might remain in the Territory so long as they behaved themselves and paid their boarding; but if they did not, they (the Mormons) would kick them to hell, where they belong."

The governor announced, upon another occasion, from the pulpit, "that he was not opposed to the government of the United States, but it was the d—d infernal corrupt scoundrels at the head of it." He applied this to Congress,

as he aftewards explained it, declaring "that the present administration had done them some justice; but no thanks to them, for it was God Almighty made them do it."

Upon another occasion two of the undersigned (Judges Brandebury and Brocchus) attended church on the Sabbath, and were invited to take seats upon the stand or platform. Secretary Harris had ceased to attend, to avoid hearing the government aspersed and denounced. Judge Brocchus had just recovered from a sick bed, and had not had an opportunity of attending church before. The preacher, Professor Spencer, of "the University of Deseret," among other expressions of ill feeling, declared that "the laws and policy of the United States government were intended to oppress the poor"—and turning his eyes upon us, in presence of this large audience, further declared, "the government of the United States is a stink in the nostrils of Jehovah, and no wonder the Mormons wish it down. We can save it by *Theocracy;* but rather that save it any other way, we will see it d—d first." Another Mormon, (Albert Carrington,) in refusing to join in firing a salute on the 4th of July, declared to Judge Brocchus and others, that the United States was going to hell as fast as it could, and the sooner the better."

This man arrived in the Territory with Judge Brocchus; is an Elder in the church, and expressed but the feelings and wishes of the residents there in sympathy with him.

These are but a few of the many seditious and hostile declarations, which it would be impossible to enumerate, made by Governor Young, and others in his presence, from the pulpit; and scarcely an opportunity was suffered to pass without aspersing the people and government of the United States, in language profane, and at times obscene. Indeed, the officers seemed to be looked upon as the mere toys of the governor's power—he treating them as he pleased, according to his capricious humor—sometimes encouraging a hope for a better [state] of affairs, to make the next outbreak of hostility and insult the more marked and humiliating.

The many important duties to be performed in the organization of the Territory, and the administration of the laws, required a cordial and confidential intercourse between the officers. The governor, however, announced soon after our arrival, in the presence of Mr. Harris and others, with great temper, "that he had ruled that people for years, and could rule them again, and he would kick any man out of the Territory who attempted to dictate to, or advise him in his duty." Under such circumstances, no communication could be had with the Executive, with any regard to self-respect, or without apprehensions of personal insult; especially as we were looked upon as offensive intruders rather than co-ordinate branches of the government.

He asked for no advice, and none was volunteered by any of us, and he was free to proceed in the performance of his duties as he thought proper.

The act of Congress required him to have a census taken, so as to apportion the number of representatives and councillors to each county; but he apportioned them without taking the census. We were informed that a census had been taken when the application was made by the State of Deseret for admission into the Union, but it was so false and exaggerated that a correct census would have betrayed the fraud. The act further required that he should fix the time and places, and appoint the persons, who should superintend the first election for councillors, representatives, and a delegate to Congress, and it prescribed the qualifications of voters, and who should be eligible to these offices. Regardless of these directions and of all forms, and in contempt of the organic act, he issued a proclamation, without the seal of the Territory or signature of the secretary, ordering the election to be held under "the provisional laws of the State of Deseret." This proclamation and many other papers were requested by the secretary, but never furnished, and, of course, no "executive record" could be made of the same. No notice was given in it as to the qualifications of voters, and those who were eligible to office, nor were any persons named to hold the elections. The consequence was, that unnaturalized foreigners officiated at the elections, voted, and were elected as representatives, and to offices not authorized by the act. The proclamation and election were a burlesque upon the order and decorum required by the organic act, and sprung from the determination of the church to do as she pleased in such matters.

He was also authorized and required, by the same act, to appoint all officers not provided for in the bill, who should continue in office until the end of the first session of the legislature. Yet there was not a sheriff, justice of the peace, or constable in the Territory legally qualified to act when we left, (excepting one or two justices of the peace appointed a few days before,) and criminals went at large untried and unpunished, so far as the United States judges could interfere. The church, as usual, punished some, as it was reported, and allowed others to go free. A few days before we left, we understood a posse of men were sent by the church in pursuit of some horse-thieves. Some of them were arrested, tried, and fined a hundred dollars, and others discharged. A man was tried in an adjoining county for an alleged offence, by a member of the church, purporting to be a judge, without a jury, and convicted and punished.

About the same time, a cold and deliberate murder was committed in the Territory upon the body of Mr. James Munroe, a citizen of the United States, from Utica, New York, on his way to Salt Lake City, by a member of the church, and the remains brought into the city and buried, without an inquest, the murderer walking through the streets afterwards under the eye of the governor, and in his society, some of the relatives of the deceased residing there, and members of the church, afraid or disinclined to act. It was reported, and believed by many, that the murder was counseled by the church, or some of its leading members; and such an impression would paralyze the hand of any one inclined to interfere. This rumor received much force from the intimacy between the offender and the leading members of the church, before and after the commission of the offence. He was several weeks in the city, and unknown, as well as his location, to any of us; it was the common talk that he intended to kill Mr. Munroe; he was permitted to go out sixty or eighty miles to meet his intended victim, and none of these men who knew the fact lifted an arm or a voice to prevent the deed. He met Munroe, who was unarmed, invited him out of his camp, took a seat and talked half an hour with him, and then rose up, bade him farewell, and blew his brains out with a pistol! We have no doubt, however, that if he had been tried, an entire acquittal would have followed, as was the result in February last, in the case of the murder of Dr. John R. Vaughan, a citizen of Indiana, then on his way to California, and the murderer suffered to go unpunished. How many other crimes and offences were punished or passed by we know not. The governor was thus true to his declaration, that "the United States judges should never try a case if he could prevent it," for we had not an officer to summon a jury, or execute a warrant, subpœna, or any kind of process, except in cases in which the United States was a party, when the marshal would be bound to act.

Congress appropriated twenty thousand dollars, to be applied under the direction of the governor and legislature in the erection of public buildings. The governor no sooner received this money than he appropriated and used every dollar of it, or a greater portion of it, in payment of debts due by the Mormon church, and in a few days after its arrival in the valley it was on its way to the United States in other hands. We were not present at its actual payment, but it was a matter of public notoriety and talked of by the gentlemen who received it. This occurred about the last of July.

Those of us then in the Territory, powerless and compelled to be observers of all these things on account of the omnipotence of the church and the governor, determined to report the facts in writing to the President of the United States. Before an opportunity for a safe transmission of such a report presented itself, one of the undersigned (Associate Chief Justice Brocchus, who arrived in the Territory on the 17th of August) addressed a large meeting of the people on the 6th of September, on behalf of the Washington Monument Association, having been commissioned by the managers thereof to ask of the people of that Territory a block of marble or other stone, to be placed in that structure, "as an offering at the shrine of patriotism." As the life, character, and services of Washington were intimately blended with everything relating to the Government and institutions of the United States, the occasion was supposed to be an appropriate one to disabuse the minds of the Mormon people of the false and prejudicial opinions they entertained towards the people and Government of the United States, and thus to arrest that flow of seditious sentiment which was so freely pouring forth from their bosoms towards the country to which they owed their highest patriotism and their best affections. We had remained there up to this period, and submitted in silence to almost every species of indignity and mortification, rather than take any step that would produce discord and involve the territorial government in difficulties. It was in this spirit that we preserved silence, until the favorable opportunity, above alluded to, was presented, when we unanimously concurred in the opinion that it was not only a matter of right, but also of duty, to have the attention of the people directed to the errors of their opinions in holding the Government of the United States and her citizens as enemies to them, and the seekers of their ruin and extermination. Such opinions were daily inculcated by the leaders of the church upon the fanatical credulity of the masses of the people. They were taught to believe that the general government sympathized with those whom they regarded as their persecutors in the States of Illinois and Missouri, and desired their overthrow and utter destruction. The natural result of such convictions was a feeling of deep-seated hostility towards the Government and people of the United States, which was every day becoming more deep and inveterate under the teachings of their spiritual leaders. We believed that to confront and remove those false impressions, thus shamefully instilled into the popular mind, would be to dry up the fountain of seditious sentiment in the Territory, and thus revive that sense of patriotism and loyalty, the manifest absence of which was then a serious obstacle to the successful operation of the territorial government, and threatened, if not corrected, to become much more serious in future. It was in pursuance of this design that the address above alluded to was made. In the course of that address the speaker endeavored, in good faith, only to correct erroneous opinions in regard to the Government from which he held his commission, without indulging in terms of invective and rebuke. His remonstrances against these opinions, and the hostile feelings resulting from them, were calm and dispassionate, and in good faith intended to effect the salutary purpose of producing peace and concord between the various branches of the Government, and good will towards the United States.

The address was entirely free from any allusions, even the most remote, to the peculiar religion of the community, or to any of their domestic or social customs. It contained not a single expression of bravado or unkindness or harsh rebuke, or any sentiment that could have been tortured into a design on the part of the speaker to inflict wantonly a wound upon the hearts of his hearers.

At the close of the address, the governor arose and denounced the speaker with great violence, as "profoundly ignorant, or wilfully wicked"—strode the stage madly—assumed various theatrical attitudes—declared he "was a greater man than ever George Washington was"—"that he knew more than ever George Washington did"—that "he was the man that could handle the sword"—and "that if there was any more discussion, there would be pulling of hair and cutting of throats." Referring to a remark of the speaker, that the United States Government was humane and kindly disposed [towards] them, he said, "I know the United States did not murder our wives and children, burn our houses, and rob us of our property, but they stood by and saw it done, and never opened their mouths, the d——d scoundrels." By this time the passions of the people were lashed into a fury like his own. To every sentence uttered, there was a prompt and determined response, showing, beyond a doubt, that all the hostile and seditious sentiments we had previously heard were the sentiments of this people.

Those of us present felt the personal danger that surrounded us. If the governor had but pointed his finger towards us, as an indication of wish, we have no doubt we would have been massacred before leaving the house. The governor declared afterwards "that if he had crooked his finger, we would have been torn to pieces."

Upon the next and succeeding days, these denunciations of the officers and the Government were renewed, as we were informed by a number of citizens, and continued in their meetings, by the governor and other leading members of the church, with increased vehemence. The Government was denounced, and the officers too, in language so vulgar and obscene, that decency would blush to hear it. We were now satisfied, that with such sentiments and feelings pervading the community, towards us and the Government, the performance of our official duties would be impracticable, and to remain and be compelled to hear these offensive and seditious denunciations, disagreeable beyond endurance. The governor had been accustomed, as many of the leading men there informed us, to enter the legislative hall, under the provisional State government, and dictate what laws should or should not be passed, and the court and jury-rooms to indicate what verdicts should be rendered, and he had given us ample evidence that he was equally omnipotent and influential with the Mormon people under the territorial government. It required no overt act, or violence, to defeat the spirit and object of the organic act, under an apparent compliance with all its requisitions. He had ordered the election of a Legislative Assembly as before described, but they were the creatures of his will, as the result shows. The other territorial officers, members of the Mormon church and under the same religious obligations, were subject to the same control. He had gone through the form of dividing the Territory into judicial districts, assigning the judges, and fixing the times for holding the courts, as one of the undersigned (Judge Branderbury) had prepared the proclamation for him. But he had declared "that the United States judges should never try a cause if he could prevent it," and it required no over act to effect this purpose. The omission to appoint proper officers to issue and execute the various writs and warrants—to summon juries, and perform other duties in the organization of courts and administration of the laws, palsied the judiciary of itself. But apart from this, we have no doubt he would have fulfilled his own prophetic declaration, by the interposition of his power as head of the church, to repel parties and business from the courts, and force them to the disposal of the church upon its own terms—screen criminals from arrest and trial—drive off witnesses and make the court a mockery and the judge an object of ridicule. They continued their proceedings in the disposal of judicial business after our arrival the same as before, regardless of the organic act, or our authority as officers. We were fully satisfied, that what was done under the organic act by the governor tardily and carelessly, was the veriest affectation and show of obedience, to secure to himself and the Mormon church the money appropriated by Congress for territorial purposes, salaries, &c. The secretary had twenty-four thousand dollars intrusted to him by the Government, for which he had given bond to the United States for its safety and faithful application to the purposes specified according to law; and efforts had been made by the governor, as we shall show, to get this money also, in addition to the twenty thousand dollars, and for the same purpose, the benefit of himself and the Mormon church.

The legislature was not to have met until January, 1852, as was given out by the governor, a period of a year and four months after the passage of the act establishing the Territory. We know not the object of this delay, unless it was his contempt for the territorial bill, and under a supposition that, as the Secretary was bound to transmit to the President and Congress on or before the first of December, annually, a copy of the executive and legislative proceedings, no exposé of the misapplication of the twenty thousand dollars appropriated for public buildings could have been made known officially before December, 1852—more than a year after it occurred. A few days after the arrival of the secretary, (19th of July,) an attempt was made, in the interview already referred to, to browbeat and intimidate him into submission to the governor's purposes, or, as the governor said, "to let the secretary know what kind of people he had to deal with"—and soon thereafter called upon him, in a patronizing manner, to borrow eight or ten thousand dollars of it for the church. He was informed by the secretary that no consideration could induce the loan of a dollar of it, as the law made an act of the kind a felony. This effort having failed, another attempt was made by setting up a claim for daily pay and mileage for the members of the last legislature of the provisional government of the "State of Deseret"—a leading member of the church informing the secretary that this money would be of great assistance to the church in relieving her from debt, and in justice should be paid as demanded. This effort having also failed, the fixed determination of the governor to get possession of the public money in the hands of the secretary for the benefit of himself and the church, revealed itself more openly and decidedly. Although the election for members of the Legislative Assembly had been held on the first Monday in August, he had made no declaration of the result of that election, as he was specifically required to do by the organic act; and without such declaration, of course the election itself was not complete. But disregarding the plain directions of the organic act in this particular, as in almost all others, he issued secret notices to members of the Legislative Assembly, to meet on Monday, the 22d day of September. The following is a *verbatim* copy of the notice sent to one of the pretended members, the original of which is now in the possession of the secretary, to wit:

"GREAT SALT LAKE CITY,
September 17, 1851.

"HON. SIR: The Legislative Assembly of Utah Territory will assemble in this city on Monday, the 22d instant, at precisely ten o'clock, a. m.

"This notice being shorter than might appear desirable, I have caused this notice to be forwarded to you, that you might not fail in attending this call.

"I have the honor to be, most respectfully and truly, yours,
"BRIGHAM YOUNG,
"*Governor of Utah Territory.*"

So solicitous was the governor that the secretary and other officers (not Mormons) should be kept in ignorance of this step, that on the 19th of September, two days after the date of the above notice, he most positively and emphatically denied, as communicated to the secretary, that any such notice had been issued. Immediately thereafter, however, on the same day, (Friday the 19th,) a proclamation, declaring the members elect, and convening the Legislative Assembly at ten o'clock on Monday, the 22d September, was brought to the secretary for his signature and seal. That proclamation, however, was never published. It should be borne in mind that the settlements in the Territory extend a distance of about three hundred miles north and south, and that some of the members of the Assembly resided two hundred and fifty miles from Salt Lake City, the place of meeting. In obedience to the secret instructions of the governor, the Legislative Assembly met on the 22d. The governor transmitted to them a printed message, which was afterwards, for some reason, suppressed, and none of the undersigned were able to procure a copy. On the 25th the secretary was served with the following paper by Mr. William Kimball, (a Mormon,) purporting to be the sergeant-at-arms of the Assembly, to wit:

"HOUSE OF REPRESENTATIVES,
"*Great Salt Lake City, Utah Territory, Sept.* 24, 1851.

"SIR: By a resolution passed by the Legislative Assembly this day, it was directed that an order be drawn on the secretary of the Territory for the sum of five hundred dollars towards defraying the incidental expenses of the Legislative Assembly.

"We therefore send this order by the sergeant-at-arms of the Legislative Council, hoping that you will furnish the same for our convenience.

"Respectfully yours, &c.,

"WILLARD RICHARDS,
"*President of the Council.*

"H. CORNEY,
"*Secretary of the Council.*

"W. W. PHELPS,
"*Speaker of the House of Representatives.*

"ALBERT CARRINGTON,
"*Clerk House of Representatives Utah Territory.*

"To the Hon. B. D. Harris,
"*Secretary of Utah Territory.*"

This paper bears upon its face evidence of an intention to get possession of the money in the hands of the secretary by any and all means. The Assembly could not have been ignorant of the obvious fact, that such an order could not be legally accepted and paid by the secretary; his duty being to pay the contingent expenses of the Legislative Council only upon the presentation of proper vouchers, showing that the expenditure had been legally incurred, was reasonable in amount, &c.; and not to furnish money in round sums to the Assembly, to be disposed of as they pleased. But more evidence of this intention to get the money remains to be told. *With the foregoing order*, Mr. Kimball, the sergeant-at-arms, placed in the hands of the secretary a copy of joint resolutions passed by the Legislative Assembly on the 24th of September, and approved by the governor, (a copy of which is herewith transmitted,) ordering and requiring the United States marshal (a Mormon) to demand this money from the secretary; and if he refused to surrender it, to seize and imprison him until he delivered over the whole amount. The marshal being absent, his deputy (Horace Eldridge, a Mormon) undertook the execution of the order. The secretary refused to comply with the demand, and transmitted his reasons therefor in writing. As Governor Young had declared he would have this money, if he had to take it by violence, the secretary applied to the supreme court for an injunction, which was granted, forbidding the marshal and others from seizing or intermeddling with the funds and other property of the United States in the custody of the secretary. It was understood the members, being all Mormons, would relinquish their daily pay and mileage to the church.

But the governor's efforts to get the money did not stop here. A warrant was issued by Aaron F. Farr, a member of the church, purporting to be a justice of the peace, but who had neither given bond nor taken the oath of office, so far as we could learn, directed "to any legal officer of the aforesaid Territory (Utah) and county of Great Salt Lake," commanding him "to restrain and to take A. W. Babbit into your possession, and also the effects of A. W. Babbit, consisting of wagons, carriages and teams, and search his wagons for a sum of money, probably gold, to the amount of twenty-four thousand dollars, and for the seal of the Territory of Utah, and bring the same before me in Great Salt Lake City, and to search all other suspected persons and places." Mr. Babbit (Honorable A. W. Babbit, late delegate in Congress from the Territory) had left the city a day or two before, with his family and household affairs, on his return to the United States. There was no one named in the warrant as complaining, no oath made, and no offence alleged. It was placed in the hands of a man, another member of the church, purporting to be a constable, but who had neither given bond nor taken an oath of office, who, with a force of thirty men or more, well armed and mounted, started in pursuit, with instructions from the governor, as we were informed, "to bring Babbit back, dead or alive." They came upon his camp about forty miles from the city, some time in the night, and in the morning Mr. Babbit and his family found themselves surrounded by a body of armed men. The carriages and wagons were emptied and the contents searched, and then reloaded to be taken back to the city. Mr. Babbit appealed to them to allow his family and teams to proceed on their journey, as a delay of a few days might overwhelm them in snow-storms, and repeated trips over the mountains he had already passed would so fatigue and break down his animals, as at that late period in the year to seriously endanger the lives of himself and family on the plains. He at the same time made known his own willingness to return with them. But their orders from the governor were peremptory, and they refused. The tent was rudely torn down over the head of his wife, then nursing a sick child, his family ordered into the carriages, and the teams turned back to the city. This extraordinary writ was executed, as above stated, *after* the injunction of the supreme court had been granted, forbidding all persons from seizing or intermeddling with the money of the United States.

Mr. Babbit applied for and was discharged from custody upon a *habeas corpus* by one of the undersigned judges. Beyond his discharge, he could procure no redress for this grievance from a Mormon community, especially as the outrage had been perpetrated by command of the governor. It may not be improper to add, in this connexion, that the secretary succeeded in keeping possession of the money, brought it over the plains, and on his arrival at St. Louis, deposited it with the Assistant Treasurer to the credit of the United States.

We deem it our duty to state, in this official communication, that polygamy, or "plurality of wives, is openly avowed and practised in the Territory, under the sanction and in obedience to the direct commands of the church." So universal is this practice, that very few if any leading men in that community can be found who have not more than one wife each. The prominent men in the church, whose example in all things it is the ambition of the more humble to imitate, have each many wives; some of them, we were credibly informed and believe, as many as twenty or thirty, and Brigham Young, the governor, even a greater number. Only a few days before we left the Territory, the governor was seen riding through the streets of the city in an omnibus, with a large company of his wives, more than two-thirds of whom had infants in their arms. It is not uncommon to find two or more sisters married to the same man; and in once instance, at least, a mother and her two daughters are among the wives of a leading member of the church. This practice, regarded and punished as a high and revolting crime in all well civilized countries, would, of course, never be made a statutory offence by a Mormon legislature; and if a crime at common law, the courts would be powerless to correct the evil with Mormon juries.

The city of Great Salt Lake is an important point in the overland route to Oregon and California, for the emigrant to replenish his stores or to winter, if overtaken by the advance of the season. But the intimidation which is produced by the denunciations and conduct of the Mormon church and people, upon citizens of the United States passing through or engaged in business there, is such, as to drive the emigrant upon another route to avoid it, and the residents to submit to all the impositions of the church to prevent a sacrifice of their business. No man dare open his mouth in opposition to their lawless exactions, without feeling its effects upon his liberty, his business, or his life. And thus, upon the soil of the United States, and under the broad folds of its stars and stripes, which protect him in his rights in every part of the civilized world, there is a spot where the citizen is brow-beaten and despoiled of his liberties as a freeman by a religious despotism. One of the undersigned (Judge Brandebury,) on his journey through the Territory, met a young man at Fort Bridger, about one hundred and twelve miles from Salt Lake City, who informed him that he had copied and forwarded to the President of the United States a letter written by James McCabe, esq., of Pontiac, Michigan, who had spent the winter in Salt Lake City, and was then on his way to Oregon, giving an account of the treatment he and others had received from the people there, and their seditious and treasonable feelings towards the United States. He stated that to give the President the facts, and conceal himself lest the Mormons should kill him if they found it out, he had signed the letter "William or George Johnston," (if remembered correctly) and thus left scarcely a mark by which an inquiry could be made into the facts. We have now before us the report of several trials which took place there before we arrived, furnished us by a respectable gentleman there at the time, and now residing in the United States, confirming the information we had received, that "gentiles" (as all are called who are not Mormons) were tried and sentenced for trivial offences to two, five, and ten years of labor upon the public highways, with ball and chain to their legs, and no shelter at night but caverns dug in the earth. We saw one of these highways cut out of the side of a mountain, and the caverns far down at its base, but the approach of the federal officers, as we were informed, was the signal for the release and banishment of these "convicts from the Territory." The account before us is too voluminous to embody in this report, but we transcribe a part of a single case, only to show the feelings there towards the government and people of the United States.

Washington Loomis was put upon trial for a larceny, and the report proceeds: "The indictment being read, defendant pleaded not guilty, when the court ordered him sworn. He testified that he knew nothing of the matter charged." George Love was then called and sworn for the prosecution, and testified "that he was positive of Loomis's innocence, for that he (Love) knew who had committed the crime, &c." Major Geo. D. Grant (a Mormon) was then called as a witness for the prosecution, for the avowed purpose of impeaching Love. He stated, that he might have to tell some hearsay statements in relating his story. Defendant's counsel, James McCabe, of Pontiac, Michigan, objected to this for two reasons: first, the prosecution had no right to impeach their own witness: second, that hearsay testimony was wholly inadmissible. Upon this Major Grant flew into a rage, and for fifteen minutes indulged in a most outrageous tirade of profanity and abusive threats towards the defendant's counsel, (Mr. McCabe,) the Government of the United States, Missouri and Illinois mobites, &c., shaking his fists over the counsel's head, and several times threatening his life; giving vent to the most settled malignity and treasonable designs towards the United States Government; declaring that this is not a civil court, but that the military rules here, and he commanded them; and that, by the Eternal God, he would call in the "legion" and "tap the claret" of this d——d villanous emissary (Mr. McCabe) of that mob Government, (United States,) sent here to spy out their liberties and frighten the court with his exceptions and technicalities, and clear d——d scoundrels from punishment, &c., &c. The cries of "amen," "we are with you," "go it," "we will back you," "to the death," "we will stand by you through blood or hell," often broke from the crowd during this exhibition of extreme patriotism and bravery; and the court highly applauded the conduct of the witness, the Chief Justice (Perkins) crying, "Amen! that is the spirit of Jesus." The hearsay evidence was admitted, the defendant convicted "as accessory after the fact," for which there was no count in the indictment, and sentenced to one year's hard labor on the public works, with ball and chain. Defendant's counsel moved for the privilege of commuting by the payment of money, as had been done to others, but motion denied. Before the defendant was arrested, all his property was seized by process from this court; his counsel filed a motion to release it, that defendant might have the use of it in his trial and defence, but the motion was overruled. The material facts we have detailed in our report are known, more or less, to many other persons, and we invite the examination of almost any "gentile" who has been there, and whose person and business are secure from danger, in proof of the seditious and treasonable feelings of the leaders in the church, towards the people and Government of the United States.

These people are now living upon the soil of the United States, and drawing their sustenance from it, free of charge. The Government is paying their governor, judges, secretary, attorney, marshal, and Indian agents—allowing them to elect their own legislature and a delegate to Congress, and paying them out of the public treasury. They have received twenty thousand dollars for public buildings, and five thousand dollars for a library; and instead of the manifestation of respect and gratitude for these manifold favors, they are inexorable in their hatred, and are ready and willing to plot the destruction of their liberal benefactor. It is impossible for any officer to perform his duty or execute any law not in sympathy with their views as the Territory is at present organized. Their conduct shows that they either disregard, or cannot appreciate, the blessings of the present form of government established for them by the United States. We have no doubt the evils complained of will suggest the remedy, and that the Government has the power and the inclination to maintain its dignity and enforce obedience and respect to the laws, upon every part of its territory where there is not patriotism enough in the people to do it.

Aware of the solicitude of the President, that the officers appointed for that Territory should so proceed in the discharge of their official duties as to secure the confidence and amicable co-operation, and promote the welfare, of the people among whom they were sent, we were not only scrupulously careful to give no cause of offence, but equally slow to take offence at any exhibition of a want of courtesy or good will towards us. In view of these considerations, we submitted in silence and remained at our posts, until the conviction was forced upon us, that to remain longer would be to forfeit not only our own self-respect, but all claim to the approbation of the Government that had honored us with its confidence.

We have the honor to be, very respectfully, sir, your ob't serv'ts,

LEMUEL G. BRANDEBURY

Chief Justice of the Supreme Court of the United States for the Territory of Utah.

PERRY E. BROCCHUS,

Associate Justice of the Supreme Court of the United States for the Territory of Utah.

B. D. HARRIS,

Secretary of the Territory of Utah.

To the PRESIDENT OF THE UNITED STATES.

Mr. Harris to Mr. Webster.

WASHINGTON, *January* 2, 1852.

SIR: I beg leave to transmit through the State Department, to the President of the United States, the accompanying papers relating to affairs in the Territory of Utah.

I have the honor to be, most respectfully, your obedient servant,

B. D. HARRIS,

Secretary of the Territory of Utah.

To the Hon. DANIEL WEBSTER,
Secretary of State of the United States.

Mr. Harris to the President of the United States.

WASHINGTON, *January* 2, 1852.

SIR: I have the honor herewith to transmit to the President of the United States, copies of papers relating to affairs in the Territory of Utah, which it was not deemed important to embody in the report recently made to the President by the officers of that Territory.

The paper marked "No. 1" is a copy of a letter placed in my hands by Mr. William Kimball, representing himself to be the sergeant-at-arms of the Legislative Assembly of the Territory, on the 25th day of September last.

The paper marked "No. 2" is a copy of preamble and resolutions also placed in my hands by Mr. William Kimball, on the same occasion above mentioned, to wit: the 25th of September.

The paper marked "No. 3" is a copy of my reply to papers marked Nos. 1 and 2, which was transmitted to the persons to whom it is addressed on the day of its date, the 25th of September.

I have also the honor to state that I have not the means of making out and transmitting to the President and to Congress, copies of the "executive proceedings" of the Territory, agreeably to the original act; the governor having neglected to file in my office many of the executive papers, although I made repeated verbal requests for them. I at length addressed to him a note, of which the following is a copy, to wit:

TERRITORY OF UTAH, SECRETARY'S OFFICE,
September 22, 1851.

SIR: Will you please send me by the bearer such executive documents as you intend to file in this office, that they may be entered upon the record, and oblige,

Very respectfully, your obedient servant,

B. D. HARRIS,
Secretary.

To his Excellency BRIGHAM YOUNG.

To this note no reply was ever received.

I have the honor to be, with the highest regard,

Your most obedient servant,

B. D. HARRIS,
Secretary of the Territory of Utah.

To the PRESIDENT OF THE UNITED STATES.

No. 1.

HOUSE OF REPRESENTATIVES, GREAT SALT LAKE CITY,
Utah Territory, September 24, 1851.

SIR: By a resolution passed by the Legislative Assembly this day, it was directed that an order be drawn on the Secretary of the Territory for the sum of five hundred dollars towards defraying the incidental expenses of the Legislative Assembly. We therefore send this order by the sergeant-at-arms of the Legislative Council, hoping that you will furnish the sum for our convenience.

Respectfully yours,

WILLARD RICHARDS,
President of the Council.
W. W. PHELPS,
Speaker H. of Reps., Utah Territory.
H. CORAY,
Secretary of Council.
ALBERT CARRINGTON,
Clerk of the House of Representatives.

To the Hon. B. D. HARRIS,
Secretary Utah Territory.

No. 2.

Joint resolution pertaining to the Secretary of Utah Territory.

Whereas the Hon. B. D. Harris, secretary of this the Territory of Utah, being about to leave, absent himself or abscond from said Territory, and intends, as we are authentically and credibly informed, to carry away or otherwise dispose of the territorial seal, records, papers, documents and property in his possession, and pertaining to his office, contrary to the organic act which provides (sec. 3) that said secretary shall reside in said Territory:

And whereas it is believed that said Secretary has in his possession the money appropriated by the act of Congress, approved February 27, 1851, amounting to $24,000, designed by Congress as compensation and mileage of members of the Legislative Assembly, and other expenses of said Territory of Utah—(see Statutes at Large, page 571, 31st Congress, 2d session:)

Whereas it is believed that said secretary should not be permitted thus to leave said Territory with so large an amount of government funds, and without having authority, which we apprehend nowhere exists, thereby seriously inconveniencing not only this Territory, but incurring the loss of said funds to the general government: therefore,

Resolved by the Legislative Council and House of Representatives in joint session assembled, That it shall be the duty of the United States marshal for said Territory to proceed forthwith and take into his possession all such papers, records, documents, and property of every kind, partaining to said office of secretary; as also all money in his possession belonging to said Territory and pertaining to said office, or intrusted by the general government, for the benefit of this Territory, in his hands, together with the seal and press of the Territory of Utah, and safely keep and preserve the same for the time being, until the Legislative Assembly shall order otherwise, or until the vacancy thus occasioned in said office shall be filled by appointment by the President of the United States, or the disabilities otherwise cease to exist.

And be it further resolved, That in case the said B. D. Harris, secretary as aforesaid, shall refuse, neglect, or anywise fail to deliver the said papers, records, seal, press, documents or money, or any other property or articles pertaining to said office, or any part thereof, then and in that case it shall be the duty of the said United States marshal for Utah Territory to arrest the said B. D. Harris, secretary as aforesaid, and him safely keep in custody until he shall comply with the foregoing resolution.

WILLARD RICHARDS,
President of the Council.
W. W. PHELPS,
Speaker of the House of Representatives.
HOWARD CORAY,
Secretary of the Council.
ALBERT CARRINGTON,
Clerk of the House of Representatives.

Approved, September 24, 1851.

BRIGHAM YOUNG,
Governor of Utah Territory

Great Salt Lake City, *September* 24, 1851.

No. 3.

Territory of Utah, Office of Secretary of State,
September 25, 1851.

Gentlemen: Your note, dated September 24th, communicating to me the substance of a resolution passed by the Legislative Assembly on the 24th instant, "directing that an order be drawn on the secretary for the sum of five hundred dollars, towards defraying the incidental expenses of the Legislative Assembly," has this day been placed in my hands by Mr. William Kimball. Being desirous that all official business transacted by me with other departments of the Government, and with individuals, should be placed in a form to be preserved, I have thought proper to communicate to you my decision, and some of the reasons which have induced it, in writing.

By the organic act of the Territory, the secretary is made the disbursing agent of the United States Government. This agency necessarily involves judicial powers to a limited extent, from which there is, and can be, no appeal except to the fountain-head. The secretary is not, in law, a mere machine, bound to allow and satisfy all claims presented to him for payment; on the contrary, he is expressly required to make diligent and minute examination as to the propriety, reasonableness, and legality of such claims and is clothed with ample powers to allow or reject the same, as his judgment shall dictate. No branch of the territorial government, executive, legislative, or judicial, can legally interfere to prevent the exercise of these powers. That the secretary is possessed of such powers, to the extent claimed, and is legally and morally bound to exercise them, is a perfectly clear and unanswerable proposition. Did I entertain any doubts on this point, my official instructions from the Treasury Department clearly and distinctly point at the propriety and necessity of the course I deem it my duty to pursue.

With these preliminary remarks, I proceed to assign, briefly, some of the reasons for the decision I am compelled to make.

1. The fourth section of the organic act of the Territory requires the governor, previous to the first election, to cause a census, or enumeration of the inhabitants of the several counties or districts of the Territory, to be taken, for the purpose of an equal apportionment of the members of the Legislative Assembly. In my judgment this provision has not been complied with, either literally or in accordance with its obvious intent and spirit. If I am correct in this opinion, of which I entertain no doubt, of course all subsequent proceedings, based upon this initiatory act, are null and void.

2. The proclamation of the governor, ordering an election, was, in my opinion, faulty both in form and substance. It did not bear the seal of the Territory or the signature of the secretary, and in other respects lacked the essentials of legal form. It was faulty in substance, in that it did not prescribe the qualifications of voters, or those to be voted for; it did not, as required by the organic act, prescribe rules and regulations for the government of the election; it did not designate the place where elections should be held, nor the persons by whom they should be conducted.

3. Aliens voted indiscriminately with American citizens, and those recognised as such by the treaty with Mexico.

4. Aliens acted as officers at the polls, and were elected to office.

5. Officers not authorized to be chosen were voted for and elected.

6. The fourth section of the organic act, before referred to, further requires the governor to declare the persons having the greatest number of votes for councillors and representatives, in the respective councillor and representative districts or precincts, to be duly elected to the Legislative Assembly. The obvious intent of the law in requiring the governor to make this declaration, was to give timely notice of an important fact to all parties interested, which includes not only the members elect themselves, but, in its narrowest signification, *all* the inhabitants of the Territory. In

fact, the election itself could not be complete until this declaration be made. It is perfectly clear that no declaration of the kind, coming within the letter or the spirit of the law, has been made; and, indeed, no declaration at all. A proclamation designed to accomplish that object was countersigned by the secretary, and attested by the seal of the Territory, on the 19th inst.; but that proclamation has never been published, or in any other manner made known to the public. But even if it had been published in legal form at the time it received the attestation of the secretary and his seal of office, it must obviously have been regarded as a nullity. No principle of law is more clearly established than that legal notices, when not expressly regulated by statute, must be specific in terms and reeasonable in time, according to the circumstances of the case. I have said that no declaration of the important fact above referred to, has been made. A printed document, purporting to be a proclamation by the governor, and to be countersigned by the secretary, bearing date September 18, 1851, declaring the members elect, and summoning the Legislative Assembly to meet in this city on Monday, September 22, 1851, has been placed in my hands. I deem it necessary to assign but a single reason why this document is as worthless, for all legal purposes, as the paper on which it is printed. It is essentially and fatally different from any executive document filed in this office, and equally so from any ever attested by the secretary or impressed with the seal of the Territory.

7. The same section of the organic act, above referred to, makes it the duty of the governor to appoint the time and place for the first meeting of the Legislative Assembly. This duty, it is plain, has never been discharged in a manner answering the requirements of law. The printed document before alluded to contains the only appointment of the kind that has been made, and that document has already been shown to be null and void.

I have thus, gentlemen, assigned seven distinct reasons for deciding, as I am now constrained to do, to allow no claim for mileage or per diem allowance to the members of the Assembly now in session, purporting to be the Legislative Assembly of the Territory of Utah, and to pay no contingent expenses connected therewith. No one can regret more sincerely than myself, that law, facts, and my official instructions and obligations, all conspire to render any other decision impossible. I may be permitted to add, however, that the just and legal rights of no one will be cancelled or in any manner prejudiced by this decision. Fortunately there is one appeal from it, and only one, to wit: to the Secretary of the Treasury, at Washington, and through him to the President of the United States, as may readily be ascertained by reference to the independent treasury act, passed 1846, and subsequent modifications thereof, prescribing the duties and responsibilities of disbursing agents. I shall myself so refer the whole matter, including a copy of this letter, for review. Should my decision be reversed, the well-known justice and liberality of the government whose agent I have the honor to be, will insure prompt reparation.

With your note, alluded to in the commencement of this paper, I also received from the hands of Mr. William Kimball a certified copy, approved by the governor, of a certain preamble and resolutions, passed on the 24th inst., by the bodies over which you respectively preside, setting forth in substance that I, the secretary of the Territory, it is believed, am about to abscond from the Territory with the public funds, and directing the United States marshal to take forcible possession of the money and other property pertaining to my office, and, in case I refuse to deliver up the money and property aforesaid, to arrest and imprison me, the secretary, until I comply.

As a faithful officer of the United States Government, to which I am alone responsible for my official conduct, I can have but one reply to make to this extraordinary demand. I most emphatically refuse to accede to it; and at the same time, deny the right of even a *legal* legislative assembly to exercise any control in the matter. To those who have the legal right to question and control my official conduct, I am, and ever shall be, at all times ready to render a faithful account of my stewardship.

In reply to the assertion, or insinuation, contained in the preamble above referred to, that I am about to *abscond* from the Territory, I have simply to express my unfeigned astonishment that honorable men should be willing to father it.

Very respectfully, your obedient servant,

B. D. HARRIS,
Secretary.

To Willard Richards and W. W. Phelps, Esqs.

Mr. Bernhisel to the President of the United States.

United States Hotel,
Washington, December 30, 1851.

Sir: On the 9th instant, I addressed to you a letter asking that "I may be informed, at the earliest convenient moment, of any allegations which the officers who had recently returned from Utah Territory may prefer, that in your judgment call for notice." On Wednesday evening, the 24th instant, I received a note from the Honorable Daniel Webster, Secretary of State, informing me that the charges of the returned officers, just referred to, were on file in the Department of State. The public offices being closed at the hour at which I received it, and the next day being Christmas, I was unable to obtain admission to the State Department before Friday, the 26th instant. Thus for the first time apprized on that day of these numerous charges, and having been on the same day informed by your Excellency that they would be communicated to the House of Representatives on Monday, the 29th instant, I cannot, of course, be expected now to make an elaborate reply to them. Nor indeed could I feel myself authorized, under any circumstances, to enter into, countenance, or admit an official discussion of either the religious faith or the moral habits of the people of Utah. But as to so much of the charges of the late officers of that Territory, against the Governor and Council thereof, as can be matter of public concern, I shall esteem it my duty, at the earliest moment, to ask for them the closest scrutiny of a Congressional committee; and, in the mean time, I take leave to place among the executive archives my prompt, unqualified, and peremptory negation of their truth.

With sentiments of great respect, I have the honor to be, your obedient servant,

JOHN M. BERNHISEL,
Delegate from Utah.

To the President of the United States.

Governor Young to the President of the United States.

Great Salt Lake City,
September 29, 1851.

Sir: It is now over one year since "An act to establish a Territorial Government for Utah" became a law of Congress. Information of this fact reached this place in November following; and about the first of January authentic information was received of the appointments of the territorial officers by the President. This news being confirmed on the third day of February, I took the oath of office as governor of this Territory, in accordance with the provisions of the organic act. Owing to the great distance from this place to the seat of the General Government, I considered it of the first importance that the preliminary arrangements for the organization of the Territory should be accomplished as soon as possible, in order that a delegate might be legally returned to the Congress of the United States before the lateness of the season should render the (at any time) long and arduous journey dangerous, if not impracticable; hence my anxiety to proceed with as little delay as possible, in obtaining the enumeration of the inhabitants, preparatory to appointing the election districts, and apportioning the members of the Council and House of Representatives to be elected from each.

Having been appointed census agent to take the census of Deseret, and, owing to the total miscarriage of instructions and blanks which had not, neither indeed have yet arrived, the taking of that census had been delayed for a season; but now being required to cause the enumeration to be taken for the use of the Territory, and despairing of the blanks coming on, I proceeded to take the census, and appointed my assistants to make out two sets of returns, one for the United States as census agent for Deseret and one for Utah, which required not the full census, but merely the enumeration of the inhabitants; this was sufficiently accomplished to enable me to make out the apportionment about the first of July, which I did, and issued my proclamation declaring the same. This being previous to the arrival of the secretary, of course his seal and signature were not attached. (See proclamation No. 1.) The reason inducing this order has been recited alone, that the election might come off in time, that whoever should be elected as delegate to Congress might be enabled to go before the inclement season should set in.

Although the appointments were made early in the fall, yet no new resident officer made his appearance until the ensuing summer, and some of them not until about the first of August.

Upon the arrival of a majority of the supreme court, I again issued my proclamation districting the Territory into three judicial districts, and assigning the judges to their several districts. This proclamation bears the impress of the seal of the Territory, and signature of Mr. Harris. (See proclamation No. 3.)

Learning to my very great regret that the secretary, Mr. Harris, and Judge Brandebury and Associate Judge Brocchus, intended to return to the United States this fall, I called upon them personally to ascertain the fact, and if possible induce them to remain. They, however, assured me it was their intention to leave, and Mr. Harris also declaring that he should carry with him all the funds in his hands for the payment of the legislative expenses of the Territory, as also the seal, records, documents, &c., pertaining to his office; plainly indicating that it was his intention to essentially vacate said office, so far as Utah was concerned, and anticipate, by leaving with the funds, the non-payment of the Legislative Assembly.

I considered this course illegal, wholly unauthorized and uncalled for by any pretext whatever; I therefore concluded that I would use all legal efforts that should seem practicable, for the retention of the property and money belonging to the United States, in the secretary's hands, designed for the use of this Territory; I therefore issued my proclamation declaring the result of the election, and convening the Legislative Assembly on the 22d of the present month. This proclamation was dated on the 18th instant, thus showing but a hurried notice; but notices had been sent previously to the members elect, and when the day arrived, all of the Council were present, and only one member of the House absent. It is but due to myself to say, that this proclamation was delayed from the fact of a misunderstanding with the secretary, that he would make out the declaration of the members elect and prepare the proclamation; which failing to do, I caused it to be done, and sent it to him for his signature and impress of the seal of the Territory, intending for him to keep the manuscript thus furnished, and return a copy suitable for publication. Much to my astonishment, he placed the seal and signature to the manuscript thus furnished, not even filing a copy for record. It was published, however. (See proclamation No. 4.)

The legislature convened in accordance therewith, with the exception of one member of the House from Iron county. The secretary did not attend to furnish a roll of the members; I therefore had this duty to perform when they were called and qualified by his honor Judge Snow.

My message was the next document in order. (See No. 5.)

On the 24th instant, the Legislative Assembly passed a joint resolution, making it the duty of the United States marshal to proceed forthwith and take into his custody all of the aforesaid funds, property, &c. (See No. 6.) This resolution was presented to Mr. Harris, as also an order for five hundred dollars, to defray the incidental expenses of the Legislative Assembly. (See No. 7.) He refused to comply with the requirements of each, (as per No. 8.)

At this time, September 26th, I addressed a note to the supreme court, who I understood were then in session, asking their opinion in regard to my duty, having reference to the organic act, which requires the governor to see that the laws are faithfully executed, and requiring the said secretary to reside in said Territory, &c. (See No. 9.)

After awaiting a reply to this note until the day fixed for their departure had far advanced, I directed the United States district attorney to file a petition, which would cause them to give their opinion—(see No. 10 for copy of petition, and No. 11 for the opinion, and answer)—having determined to abide the decision of the judges. I accordingly stayed all further proceedings, and on yesterday, the 28th, I understand the secretary, Mr. Harris, and the two judges, Mr. Brandebury and Mr. Brocchus, left this city on their return to the United States.

For a reply to Mr. Harris's decision (No. 8.) I refer you to file No. 12.

Thus, sir, I have given you a plain, unvarnished tale of all our proceedings pertaining to governmental affairs, with the exception of report upon Indian affairs, which will be made to the proper department.

If your Excellency will indulge me in a few remarks, I will proceed and make them.

Mr. Harris informed me, in a conversation which I had with him, that he had *private instructions, designed for no eye but his own,* to watch every movement and not pay out any funds unless the same should be *strictly legal, according to his own judgment.*

The supreme court organized and held a session, as will appear by reference to the certified copy of proceedings (No. 13,) without waiting for the legislative authority fixing the time; and apparently having no other object than to shield and protect Mr. Harris, in leaving with the funds and property designed for the use and benefit of this Territory.

It has been said of myself, and the people over whom I have the honor to preside, that they frequently indulge in strictures upon the acts of men who are intrusted with governmental affairs, and that the government itself sometimes does not wholly escape. Now, sir, I will simply state what I know to be true—that no people exists who are more friendly to the government of the United States, than the people of this Territory. The constitution they revere, the laws they seek to honor. But the non-execution of those laws in times past for our protection, and the abuse of power in the hands of those intrusted therewith, even in the hands of those whom we have supported for office, ever betraying us in the hour of our greatest peril and extremity, by withholding the due execution of laws designed for the protection of all the citizens of the United States—it is for this we have cause for complaint, not the want of good and wholesome laws; but the execution of the same, in the true meaning and spirit of the constitution.

The foregoing is a case in point. What good and substantial reason can be given, that the people of this Territory should be deprived, for probably near a year to come, of a supreme court, of the official seal of a secretary of state, of the official publication of the laws, and other matters pertaining to the office of secretary?

Is it true that officers coming here by virtue of an appointment by the President, have *private instructions* that so far control their actions as to induce the belief that their main object is not the strict and legal performance of their respective duties, but rather to *watch* for *iniquity,* to catch at shadows, and make a man "an offender for a word;" to spy out our liberties, and, by manifold misrepresentation, seek to prejudice the minds of the people against us? If such is the case, better, far better would it be for us, to live under the organization of our provisional government, and entirely depending upon our own resources, as we have hitherto done, until such time as we can be admitted as a State, than thus to be tantalized with the expectation of having a legal government, which will extend her fostering care over all her offspring. In infancy, if ever, it is necessary to assist the rising State.

If it be true that no legal authority can be exercised over a co-ordinate and even a subordinate branch of the government, by the legislature thereof, then indeed we may expect the harmony of government to be interrupted, to hear the discordant sounds of irresponsible and law-defying agents desecrating by *their acts* the *very name* of *American* liberty.

In the appointment of new officers, if you will pardon me for making a suggestion, I would propose that such men be selected as will reside within the Territory, or have a general and extended knowledge of men and things, as well as of the elementary and fundamental principles of law and legislation; men who have lived and practised outside as well as indoors, and whose information extends to the duties of a justice of the peace, as well as the well-known passages and districts of the court-room. In relation to our present unfortunate position, pertaining to the supreme court, I can only hope that early the ensuing season we may be favored with a quorum.

As regards the funds, if an arrangement could be made authorizing Mr. Livingstone, a merchant in this place, to receive the money appropriated to meet the legislative expenses, he would most probably make such advances as might be necessary, after being advised of the privilege of so doing.

The Legislative Assembly are yet in session; of their acts and doings I shall take the liberty of making report, the same as would have been the duty of the secretary had he remained. I cannot conceive that it can or ought to be in the power of any subordinate officer to subvert, or even retard for any length of time, the ordinary motion of the wheels of government; although I am equally satisfied that it was, and is, the intention of a portion of those aforesaid officers to utterly subvert and overthrow this government of Utah; but of this I have no fears, as I know they can have no good and sufficient apology for the course they have and are pursuing.

The money that was appropriated for the year ending the 30th of June, 1851, should have been used to defray the expenses of the legislature of '50 and '51; and the government might have been organized, had the officers have been as efficient in coming here as they are now in going away. The legislature can now, as heretofore, do without their compensation and mileage, and find themselves; they were all unanimously elected (with one exception,) as was our delegate to Congress, the honorable John M. Bernhisel.

We have sought to obtain an authorized government, and the people have been well satisfied with the government in regard to all their acts in relation thereto, so far as I am acquainted; and if the men appointed had endeavored to be active in the discharge of their duties, all would have been well. Mr. Harris takes exceptions to every thing that has been done. Did he take hold, upon his arrival at this place, and endeavor to assist in the organization of this government as a secretary should do? Not at all; never was he the man to do the first thing, either by suggestion or otherwise, unless perhaps it was occasionally to set his hand and seal of the Territory to some document that had been prepared for him. Have either of the judges who are returning ever done any thing towards the organization of the Territory? They organized the supreme court chiefly, as I think, to assist Mr. Harris in leaving with the funds; and I believe Judge Branderbury appointed a clerk of the district. Judge Brocchus had determined on returning this fall, previous to his arrival, as I am credibly informed; and they both leaving at this time, just when the time has arrived for them to act, postpones indefinitely all courts in their respective districts. Judge Brocchus has *never been in his district*, that I know of. Thus, so far as the public interests are concerned, it would have been quite as well if neither of these gentlemen or Mr. Harris had ever troubled themselves to cross the plains.

Whatever may be your decision upon all these matters, be assured that it is and has been my intention to discharge faithfully every duty pertaining to my office; and that I shall receive very gratefully any instructions that you will please to give. Awaiting most anxiously to hear from you,

I have the honor to be, your Excellency,

Very respectfully and truly yours,
BRIGHAM YOUNG.

To his Excellency MILLARD FILLMORE,
President of the United States of North America.

Memorial signed by members of the Legislative Assembly of Utah to the President of the United States.

GREAT SALT LAKE CITY, *September* 29, 1851.

To Millard Fillmore, President of the United States of North America:

The undersigned, members of the Legislative Assembly for the Territory of Utah, do hereby most respectfully beg leave to show, that whereas two of the honorable justices of the supreme court of the United States for the Territory of Utah, and the Hon. B. D. Harris, secretary of the Territory, have removed from the Territory of Utah, and consequently vacated their offices within the same, therefore your memorialists do most earnestly solicit and pray the Chief Executive of the United States to fill those vacancies as speedily as possible.

Accumulated influences of a disagreeable nature may be regarded as our apology for trespassing upon the attention of our highly honored Chief Magistrate at this time. The vacating of important public offices in a manner as unwarranted as it is unprecedented, at this peculiar crisis of our colonial settlement and government, have created mingled sensations of an extraordinary character, which we wish, briefly, to pour into the bosom of the national Executive.

Immediately consequent upon the settlement of this colony, a large and heterogeneous emigration followed upon our heels, remaining here a shorter or longer time, imperatively requiring the establishment of an efficient government for the speedy protection of life, peace, virtue, and property. In addition to a transient and ungovernable emigration, almost constant Indian depredations have pleaded, like the irresistible maw of death, for the institution of some formidable order and power of government among us. A provisional government was accordingly formed, which has met the exigencies of the people, and secured general tranquillity, order, and satisfaction. And when the announcement of a territorial government under your fostering hand reached us, it was hailed with shoutings and firing of cannon. But, sir, the officers appointed sufficiently early to have reached here last winter did not arrive till July last, when measures had been taken by the governor of Utah for taking the census, and securing an election of a delegate to Congress, and members of the legislature, without the seal of the honorable secretary of the Territory. And now, in the very dawn of the arrival of the government officers, and of our hopes of an efficient territorial government, we are most seriously embarrassed with their unprovoked departure from the limits of the Territory, taking with them the judiciary, the public seal, and the public fund, leaving us in a more crippled condition, if possible, than previous to their arrival; thereby tantalizing a people of more than Spartan integrity and fortitude, that have long been struggling against the most invincible difficulties. The first demand upon the honorable secretary for stationery, desks, and such contingent expenses as might necessarily accrue in the outset of a legislative assembly, has been peremptorily refused. Not only so, but all the authorities of the Territory, including the governor and both houses of the Assembly, and marshal, have been set at naught, as exercising their functions illegally and unconstitutionally. (See document marked No. 8.) Thus, sir, when we have looked for the fostering aid of such a functionary as the honorable secretary, and for a fellow-citizen worthy the honor conferred by our illustrious Chief Magistrate, we have been annoyed with the technics of legal quackery, and our respectful address for stationery, &c., has been responded to, not as to legislators of the undivided choice and sole representation of a sovereign people, who know the right of franchise and of self-government, under the constitution, but as to men who ape authority that does not belong to them. Although we are *ipso facto* honored with the choice of a sovereign, and free people to be their representatives in legislative assembly, and the refusal of a captious stranger to accredit us with the fact does not shake the truth; still a studious violation of etiquette, when it is designed to convey burlesque, contempt, and indignity upon a legislative body, is calculated to alienate a people from such functionaries.

Your memorialists, being aware of the difficulty of sending men from the States to fill the vacancies that have accrued from the removal of the two honorable judges, and the Hon. B. D. Harris, during the period of many months to come, and feeling cautious against any possible future removals like those which now embarrass us with the want of a Territorial seal and funds, to meet constantly accruing expenses, and also the want of a full supreme court of the United States for Utah Territory, and desirous to dwell in peace and unfeigned loyalty to the constitution and general government of the United States, do therefore pray our highly honored Chief Magistrate to appoint men to fill the aforesaid vacancies, by and with the consent of the Senate, who are indeed residents among us, in order that we may enjoy the full administration of every department of government speedily, as the prosperity of the Territory shall require; and your memorialists, as in duty bound, will ever pray.

WILLARD RICHARDS, *President of Council.*

A. L. Lamereaux,	Heber C. Kimball,
John Stoker,	David H. Wells,
Gideon Brownell,	Aaron Johnson,
James Brown,	Alexander Williams,
David B. Dille,	Isaac Morley,
James G. Browning,	Jno. S. Fullmer,
David Evans,	Charles R. Dana,
William Miller,	Orson Spencer,
Levi W. Hancock,	Mr. Phelps,
Charles Shumway,	Lorin Farr,

George A. Smith.

WELFA WOODRUFF, *Speaker H. R.*

Nathaniel H. Felt,	Daniel Spencer,
David Fullmer,	Phineas Richards,
Albert P. Rockwood,	B. F. Johnson,
Edwin D. Woolly,	Hosea Stout,
Jos. Young,	H. G. Sherwood.

www.ingramcontent.com/pod-product-compliance
Lightning Source LLC
LaVergne TN
LVHW010743120826
845150LV00009B/2280

* 9 7 8 1 4 1 8 1 9 4 9 9 4 *